# SHORTLINES & INDUSTRIAL RAILROADS OF NEW JERSEY

*From the Camera & Collection of Thurlow C. Haunton Jr.*

by
**Benjamin L. Bernhart**

edited by
**Jay Leinbach**
**Melissa D. Bernhart**
**Dr. John H. L. Bernhart**
**William J. McKelvey,** NJ Transportation Heritage Center

*Along the Historic Reading Main Line*

Copyright 2007 Outer Station Project
Outer Station Project, 1335 Railroad Road, Dauberville, PA 19533
OSPpublications@aol.com     (610) 916-2433

Dedicated to

# *Thurlow C. Haunton Jr.*

An avid railfan who captured on film many of the obscure rail treasures that were found in the state of New Jersey during the years that followed World War II. I sincerely thank you for sharing your photographs and knowledge with myself and the community.

# Table of Contents

Contents of Volume I. . . . . . . . . . . . . . . . . . . . . iv
Author's Preface. . . . . . . . . . . . . . . . . . . . . . . . v
About the Author. . . . . . . . . . . . . . . . . . . . . . . vi
Publications by the OSP. . . . . . . . . . . . . . . . . . vii
Introduction by Thurlow C. Haunton Jr. . . . . . . . . . viii

American Bridge Company. . . . . . . . . . . . . . . . . . . . . 73
American Cyanamid Company. . . . . . . . . . . . . . . . . . . 75
Barber Asphalt Company. . . . . . . . . . . . . . . . . . . . . . 77
Hoboken Manufacturers Railroad. . . . . . . . . . . . . . . . . 78
Hydraulic Press Brick Company. . . . . . . . . . . . . . . . . . 88
International Smelting & Refining Company / Raritan Copper Works. . . . . 89
Koppers Coke / Seaboard By Product Coke Company. . . . . . . 94
John Dustin's War Surplus. . . . . . . . . . . . . . . . . . . . . 95
Long Beach Island Railroads. . . . . . . . . . . . . . . . . . . . 96
North Jersey Quarry Company / Lakewood Sand Company
       Porrier & McLane Contractors. . . . . . . . . . . . . . . . 104
Mount Hope Mineral Railroad. . . . . . . . . . . . . . . . . . . 105
Morristown & Erie Railroad. . . . . . . . . . . . . . . . . . . . 106
New York Ship Building Company. . . . . . . . . . . . . . . . 118
Port Reading Creosote. . . . . . . . . . . . . . . . . . . . . . . 119
R. Hollingshead Company. . . . . . . . . . . . . . . . . . . . . 120
Rahway Valley Railroad. . . . . . . . . . . . . . . . . . . . . . 121
Raritan River Sand Company. . . . . . . . . . . . . . . . . . . 132
Sandy Hook Proving Grounds. . . . . . . . . . . . . . . . . . . 133
Sayre & Fisher. . . . . . . . . . . . . . . . . . . . . . . . . . . . 135
Standard Oil Company of New Jersey / Bayway Refinery. . . . . 136
US Army / Fort Dix. . . . . . . . . . . . . . . . . . . . . . . . . 137
Warren Foundry & Pipe Company. . . . . . . . . . . . . . . . . 138
Additional Builder's Photographs. . . . . . . . . . . . . . . . . 139

# Volume I Contents

Crossman Company
East Jersey Railroad & Terminal Company
Raritan River Railroad
Union Transportation Company

# Author's Preface

Although I was introduced to the Reading Railroad at a very young age, I was not exposed (in any large degree) to the rich history of railroading in the state of New Jersey until I began researching for my publication documenting the stations and structures of the Central Railroad of New Jersey. Since that publication was released, my knowledge of New Jersey rails has greatly broadened. This knowledge has been shared with the public in several different publications. In the fall of 2006, I compiled and published a detailed history of the Hoboken Manufacturers Railroad, also referred to as the Hoboken Shore Railroad.

Enjoying and approving of the Hoboken Shore Railroad publication, Thomas C. Haunton, the son of Thurlow C. Haunton, Jr., reached out to me to share his father's collection of photographs which were either taken by himself or collected over the years. The first time I previewed the Haunton collection I was overwhelmed by its sheer size. What is present within this publication is only a small portion of the collection. Mr. Haunton had purchased or acquired numerous photographs from other sources, but few of the acquired photographs were used in this publication with the exception of official builder's photographs.

Fortunately for myself, Mr. Haunton had spent hours in compiling a detailed index to the entire collection, documenting location, date and historical information about each photograph. So often past photographers never recorded this information and it became lost or forgotten. Mr. Haunton's index of several hundred pages became the major source of the technical and historical data found within this publication.

Sincere gratitude is given to Thomas C. Haunton for the work in preparing his father's collection to be accessed and digitized for this publication. I must also thank Jay Leinbach, Dr. John H.L. Bernhart, Melissa Bernhart, and William J. McKelvey from the New Jersey Transportation Heritage Center for devoting hours to edit and proofread this publication. Lastly, I must thank you, the reader, for purchasing this book, for without your support, there would be no reason for this publication. With your support there will be many more to come.

*Benjamin L. Bernhart*
*Dauberville, PA*
*July 7, 2007*

# Want To Get Published?

The Outer Station Project is a full service publishing firm which offers authors or photographers a chance to get their works published. We help authors or photographers get started and guide them through the complex world of printing, distribution and marketing. The Outer station Project is currently looking for authors or photographers for future publications. Best of all, you keep the copyright to your works. The Outer Station Project has access to the latest digital technology and can transform your photograph collection into a digital library for future generations. I look forward to hearing from you.

# About the Author

Benjamin L. Bernhart first became interested in railroads as he was growing up along the abandoned Schuylkill & Lehigh Branch of the Reading Company. His interest was further fostered during the Bernhart family trips to visit relatives within the city of Reading, Pennsylvania. A drive along Sixth Street, paralleling the Reading Railroad shops, was a routine event. At the young age of fourteen, Mr. Bernhart began his railroad career as a volunteer on the Wanamaker, Kempton & Southern Railroad.

As a teenager Benjamin L. Bernhart moved to the city of Reading, graduating from Reading High School in 1991. During his high school senior year, Benjamin wrote his first publication entitled *The Outer Station, Reading, Pennsylvania*. In 1993, he was awarded a prestigious research fellowship from the Hagley Museum & Library, spending a summer researching the letter books of G.A. Nicolls, the first general superintendent of the Philadelphia & Reading Railroad. Mr. Bernhart attended Albright College and graduated from its Honors Program with a BA in History. Serving as an historical consultant, Mr. Bernhart has been employed by the City of Reading and the Lancaster County Planning Commissions to conduct historical research into rail transportation within those governmental jurisdictions.

Upon graduation Benjamin Bernhart followed his career dream by obtaining a position with the Pennsylvania Historic Museum Commission at the Railroad Museum of Pennsylvania. During this time, he was also employed by the Strasburg Rail Road. Due to family commitments, Mr. Bernhart returned to the city of Reading in 1997 and continued to author publications, receiving in 1999 the "Outstanding Citizenship Award" from the mayor of Reading for his work in preserving the heritage of the city. In 1990 Mr. Bernhart was also honored with the title "Reading Company Historian" by Reading Company president, James Wunderly.

Benjamin L. Bernhart currently sits on the Board of Trustees of the Historical Society of Berks County and will be guest curator for their major exhibit honoring the Reading Railroad's 175th anniversary in 2008. He is also a member of the Friends of the Railroad Museum of Pennsylvania. Mr. Bernhart has written nearly thirty publications and numerous articles. He currently works as an independent historian, with his office located along the historic Main Line of the Reading Railroad. For information on hiring Mr. Bernhart, please write to him at: 1335 Railroad Road, Dauberville, PA 19533, call him at (610) 916-2433 or email him at OSPpublications@aol.com.

# Publications Available

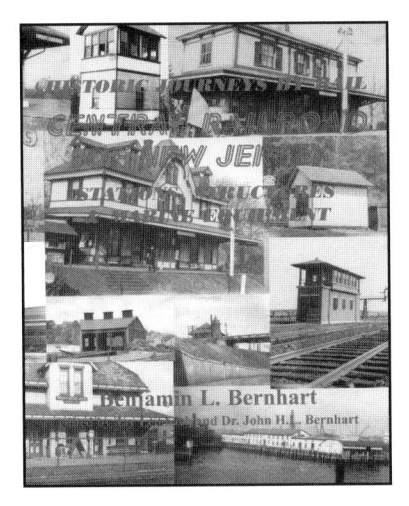

**Outer Station Project**
1335 Railroad Road, Dauberville, PA 19533
(610) 916-2433 OSPpublications@aol.com

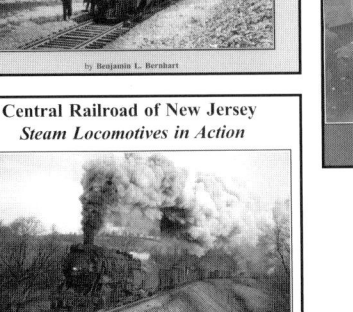

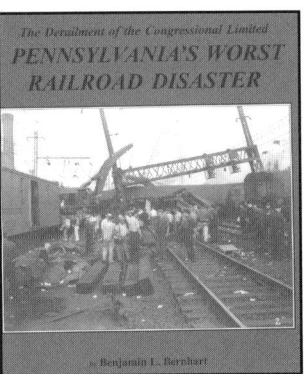

**Hoboken Shore Railroad**
*28 pages, 44 b&w Illustrations, Soft Cover, SRP $10.00*

**North Broad Street Station, Volume 1**
*28 pages, 67 b&w Illustrations, Soft Cover, SRP $10.00*

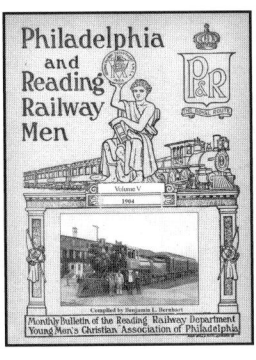

**Pennsylvania Railroad in the Schuylkill River Valley**
*168 pages, color and b&w Illustrations, Hard Cover, Out of Print*

**Central Railroad of New Jersey Steam Locomotive in Action**
*48 pages, 70 b&w Illustrations, Soft Cover, SRP $12.00*

**Reading Railroad Steam in Action, Volume II**
*72 pages, 116 b&w Illustrations, Soft Cover, Out of Print*

**Historic Journeys by Rail: Central Railroad of New Jersey Stations, Structures & Marine Equipment**
*168 pages, 637 b&w Illustrations, Soft Cover, SRP $30*

**Michigan Rail Disasters 1900-1940**
*160 pages, Nearly 200 b&w Illustrations, Soft Cover, SRP $34.95*

**Shortlines & Industrial Railroads of New Jersey, Volume I**
*80 pages, 175 b&w Illustrations, Soft Cover, SRP $24.95*

**Philadelphia & Reading Railway Men Magazines, 1904**
*Reproductions of the 1904 Employee Magazines, Out of Print*

**Reading - Jersey Central Magazine, Vol 1, Issues 1-6, 1936**
*208 pages, Numerous b&w Illustrations, Soft Cover, LE, SRP $30*

**Reading - Jersey Central Magazine, Vol 1, Issues 7-12, 1937**
*208 pages, Numerous b&w Illustrations, Soft Cover, LE, SRP $30*

**New York & Long Branch: A Photographic Rememberance**
*40 pages, 76 Color and b&w Illustrations, Soft Cover, SRP $17.95*

**Covered Bridges of Reading & Berks County**
*80 pages, 76 b&w Illustrations, Soft Cover, Out of Print*

**Hurricane Agnes: Great Floods of Reading and Berks County**
*64 pages, 88 Color and b&w Illustrations, Soft Cover, SRP $20*

**The Derailment of the Congressional Limited**
*32 pages, 67 b&w Illustrations, Soft Cover, SRP $12*

# Introduction

My interest in railroads started when I was in grammar school. I grew up in the northern New Jersey town of Long Branch, one block away from the main passenger station, and directly across from the rail crossing at Bath Avenue. The crossing was tended 24 hours a day, with manually operated gates to be raised and lowered each time a train approached, which happened frequently. The station was served by the New York and Long Branch Railroad, a combination of the Pennsylvania Railroad serving Penn Station in New York City and the Central Railroad of New Jersey running into Jersey City, where passengers transferred to a ferryboat to complete the trip into New York.

Long Branch also had a freight station across the way, resulting in a yard full of freight cars waiting for their contents to be unloaded. The cars had the initials of the railroad of origin, whose name was not always spelled out. In the grammar school library, I found a collection of Official Railway Guides which listed all the US railroads – where they ran and how long each was. Using the guides, I started looking up those whose name I did not know and tracing them. I noticed that many were short lines and some were in New Jersey. For my birthday I asked my parents for a copy of one of the railway guides. They in turn told my grandparents, who gave me a copy of the November 1942 guide – still in my possession. My hobby had started. With this new acquisition I proceeded to list those in New Jersey near enough to visit. I decided on the Union Transportation Company between Hightstown and Pemberton, to be followed by the Raritan River in South Amboy, the East Jersey Railroad and Terminal in Bayonne, and the Hoboken Manufacturers in Hoboken.

I was sixteen in April 1945 when I took my first trip to see the UT. On later trips, I'd occasionally meet up with those I corresponded with through Railroad Magazine's "Switch List" – Bill Young for the Rahway Valley Railroad, Tom Taber for the Morristown and Erie, Jay Wolfson for the Raritan River Railroad, and John Brinckmann for the Union Transportation Company and the Tuckerton Railroad. Since none of us had cars in those days, I'd arrange to meet each at some pre-arranged spot, traveling by train, bus, or hitchhiking. Most of my trips, though, were on my own. My library's copy of the New Jersey WPA Guide showed me much about the state's highway system, which I found I could use getting around to the different railroads.

My hobby progressed during my high school, junior college, and college years, mostly on vacations. I would often take the train up to South Amboy (along with my bike) and ride around the Raritan River Railroad, then pop my bike back on the train later and head home. Nobody ever stopped me and I had free access wherever I would go, although I usually did ask permission first.

After I graduated from college, I got a job with Standard Brands in Hoboken, N.J. which was served by the Hoboken Manufacturers Railroad, one of the short lines I used to photograph. Living in Hoboken during the week, I commuted back to Long Branch often on weekends or visited other short-line railroads. Railroads were interrupted for two years between 1951 and 1953 while I served in the army during the Korean War. An irony for me was that our rifle range road during basic training at Fort Dix was over the right of way of the military railroad I had seen on one of my trips to the Union Transportation Company years before.

When I returned from Korea, I married and started to raise a family. I resumed my railroad trips, and frequently took my family along. One of my favorite railroads was the Raritan River and I got to know many of the engineers quite well. Other favorites were the Union Transportation Company in New Egypt and the abandoned Tuckerton Railroad, visits to both made easier when my family and I relocated to South Jersey.

I've spent many an hour tramping over tracks and trestles, going from engine to engine, taking photos and writing down numbers, then running back to the car and chasing the engine to its next destination. I continue to do it to this day!

The photographs for this book taken by me were shot between 1945 and 1966, while the builder's photographs were acquired over my sixty-plus years as a collector.

*Thurlow C. Haunton, Jr.*
*June 2007*

# The American Bridge Company

Business tycoon J.P. Morgan organized the consolidation of twenty-eight steel fabricators and constructors to form the American Bridge Company in April, 1900. The company's headquarters was located in Coraopolis, Pennsylvania and the nearby town of Ambridge was a typical company town. The company developed many techniques in the advancement of steel construction, leading to the fabrication and construction of bridges, buildings, ships, and many other products. From its organization, American Bridge has operated on a national and international level. To meet the demand for its products, several facilities were needed. Trenton, New Jersey was home to one of these facilities.

*Left:* American Bridge Co. 0-6-0 saddle tank 4 was built by the Baldwin Locomotive Works (Builder's number 2886) in August, 1906. (Baldwin Locomotive Works Builder's Photo.)

*Above:* The American Locomotive Company (Builder's number 44265) constructed this 0-6-0T, locomotive 7, at the ex-Pittsburgh Locomotive and Car Works in July of 1910. (ALCO Builder's Photo.)

***Top:*** *Another Baldwin Locomotive Works product (Builder's number 54807), American Bridge Company engine 13, joined the roster in May of 1921. ( Baldwin Locomotives Works Builder's Photo.)*  ***Bottom:*** *In 1917 a smaller saddle tank locomotive, 0-4-0T number 16, was purchased from ALCO. This locomotive was built at the ex-Cooke Locomotive & Machine Works in Paterson, New Jersey. (ALCO Builder's Photo.)*

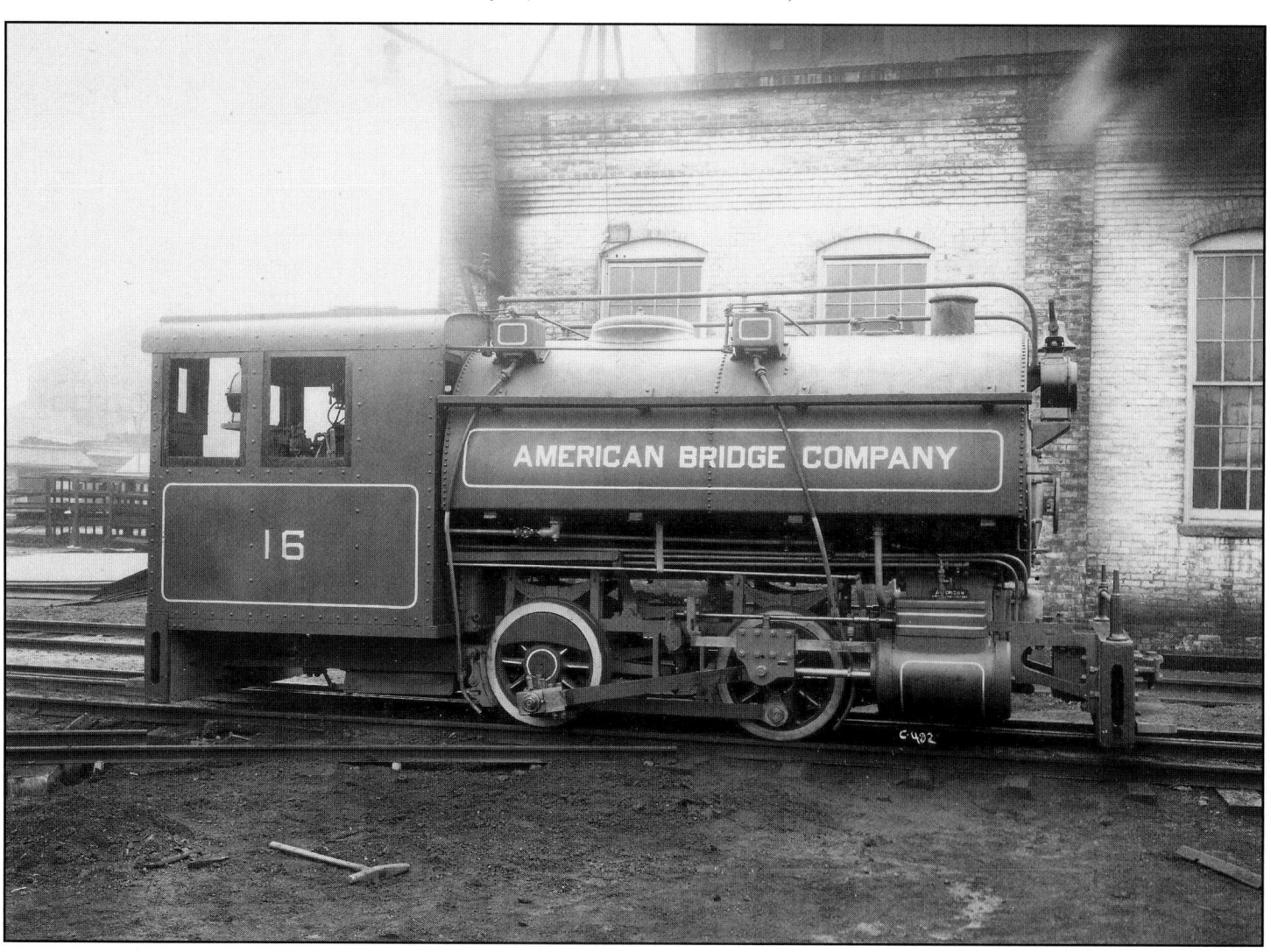

# The American Cyanamid Company

The American Cyanamid Company processed and manufactured chemicals at a facility in Bound Brook, New Jersey since before World War I. By 1980, the facility encompassed approximately 575 acres and was bounded by the Raritan River, Interstate 287, and New Jersey Route 28. Over the years more than 800 different chemicals were produced at this facility. Due to economic pressure the company was forced to shut down. During the golden age of rail transportation, the American Cyanamid Company maintained a fleet of switching locomotives.

*Above:* *The first locomotive to be purchased by American Cyanamid Company was this little 0-4-0 saddle tank engine manufactured by ALCO at their Rogers facility in Paterson, New Jersey, in 1913. ( ALCO Builder's Photo.)*

*Above:* *ALCO built this 0-6-0 at the ex-Cooke Locomotive and Machine Works plant, Paterson, New Jersey, in 1917. Note the interesting design of locomotive 10's tender. (ALCO Builder's Photo.).*

***Top & Middle:*** Two views of American Cyanamid Company diesel locomotive 13. The diesel locomotive was built by Baldwin Locomotive Works in 1946. (Baldwin Locomotive Works Builder's Photo.)

***Bottom:*** Six years after diesel locomotive 13 joined the American Cyanamid Company motive power roster, another Baldwin diesel was purchased. This new diesel was numbered 14. (Baldwin Locomotive Works Builder's Photo.)

# The Barber Asphalt Company

Shortly after the Civil War concluded, cities once again began to grow and industries and inventors looked for ways to improve the transportation infrastructure. One such improvement was the advent of road paving with asphalt. Asphalt paving was superior to dirt or cobblestone streets. One of the forefathers of asphalt paving was Edward J. DeSmeldt, who was granted seven patents in 1870 and 1871. Several other prominent businessmen saw the opportunity and the potential profit which could be made by forming asphalt companies. One of these men was William Averell from New York. Mr. DeSmeldt became aware of Mr. Averell's activity and filed infringement suits against him in 1880.

Two other businessmen, Amazi L. Barber and James McLain, took interest in the legal battle between Edward DeSmeldt and William Averell. An out-of-court settlement was reached in the spring of 1880. This settlement laid the foundation for the formation of the American Asphalt Pavement Company on April 21, 1880. A complicated exchange of stock and capital between all parties took place. William Averell became president, Amazi L. Barber was appointed head of the executive committee, and Edward J. DeSmeldt and James McLain served as executive committee members.

Within a year, daily disagreements and heated arguments between the executive committee members and Mr. Averell were routine. This turmoil led Amazi Barber to separate himself from the American Asphalt Paving Company to form his own company known as the Barber Asphalt Paving Company, with a facility in Perth Amboy, New Jersey.

In 1883, William Averell filed suit against Mr. Barber. After fifteen years of legal maneuvering, Mr. Averell was awarded a $700,000 judgement. Amazi L. Barber carried on and the Barber Asphalt Paving Company became a national force in the paving industry. In 1938, the name was changed to Barber Asphalt Company. The name was again changed to the Barber Oil Corporation. Combining with the Standard Oil Company of California in 1946, the company became the American Gilsonite Company, which brought the Barber name to an end.

*Above:* Barber Asphalt locomotive 7 operated at the Perth Amboy, NJ facility. The engine was built by the Baldwin Locomotive Works (Builder's number 59889) in March of 1927. The locomotive was later sold to the Federal Shipbuilding & Dry Dock Company in South Kearny, New Jersey. In January, 1955, the engine was sold for scrap. (Baldwin Locomotive Works Builder's Photo.)

# The Hoboken Manufacturers Railroad / The Hoboken Shore Railroad

The history of this tiny switching railroad is one of mystery. On September 17, 1895, several local businessmen, including descendants of Colonel John Stevens, incorporated the Hoboken Railroad Warehouse and Steamship Connecting Company. This railroad operated under the nickname "Hoboken Shore Road" due to its closeness to the shores of the New York Harbor. Seven years later the Hoboken Manufacturers Railroad was incorporated on July 21, 1902. The American Warehouse & Trading Company was incorporated on November 20, 1905, and soon thereafter took control of the Hoboken Manufacturers Railroad. Less than a year later, on June 19, 1906, the Hoboken Manufacturers Railroad leased the Hoboken Railroad Warehouse & Steamship Connecting Company. The purpose of the railroad was to serve the many factories and dockside warehouses that had sprung up along the western bank of the Hudson River in Hoboken.

The Hoboken Railroad Warehouse & Steamship Connecting Company began operations in 1897. The railroad received and sent its traffic by means of its interchange with the Erie Railroad in Weehawken, New Jersey. This interchange point was the railroad's northern terminus. The railroad then stretched southward approximately one half mile along the waterfront. The railroad grew quickly and within several years it contained numerous yard tracks and several industrial spurs to the local factories and warehouses. An interchange with the Delaware, Lackawanna & Western Railroad was created with the construction of a pier that could accept carfloats at the foot of Eleventh Street in Hoboken.

The Hoboken Railroad Warehouse & Steamship Connecting Company was constructed as an electrified railroad with the wire installed at a height of twenty-two feet, the standard for electrified steam railroads. Due to its nature as a switching railroad, it was necessary for brakemen to stand on the top of freight cars while they were in motion. This explains the height of the wires. Three General Electric steeple cab electric motors, one Baldwin Locomotive Works electric motor, and two modified interurban trolley cars soon found their way onto the railroad's roster.

There is a common misconception that when the Federal Government seized German Trans-Atlantic Shipping Company piers and property in Hoboken during War World I in 1917, they also seized the Hoboken Manufacturers Railroad. The railroad was not seized, but purchased when the Federal Government purchased all the stock of the American Warehouse & Trading Company on July 1, 1917. The exact federal agency which ran the railroad during World War I is unclear. The United States Railroad Administration or the war department may have controlled the railroad. After the war, the railroad was not sold to private ownership but was managed by the United States War Department. The US War Department managed the railroad for many more years. During this time Brigadier General George F. Downer was in charge of the railroad. One of his main contributions to the railroad was that of acquiring at least two Army

**Right:** *A postcard depicting motor No. 1. (Collection of Thurlow C. Haunton, Jr.*

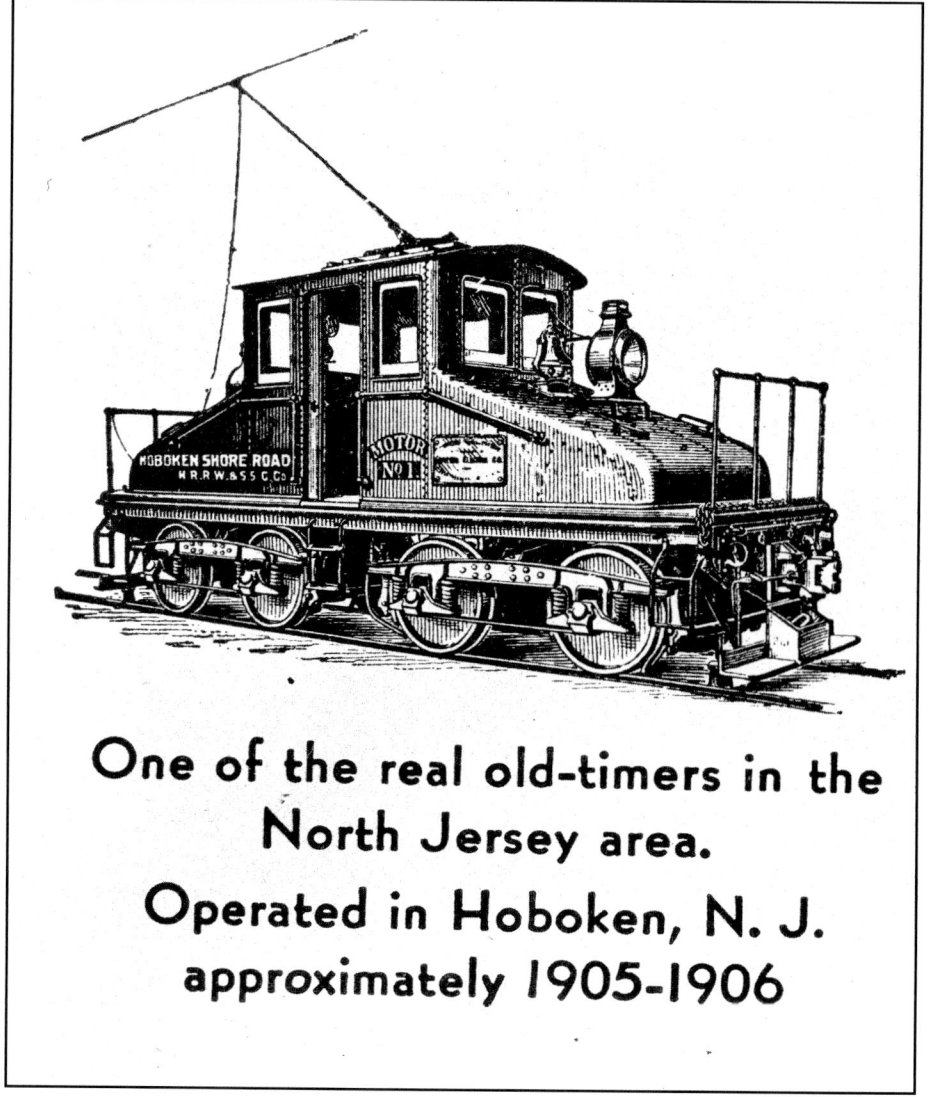

One of the real old-timers in the North Jersey area. Operated in Hoboken, N. J. approximately 1905-1906

owned steam locomotives. Unfortunately, information about and photographs of these steam locomotives on the Hoboken Manufacturers Railroad are extremely rare. In fact, this publication may contain the only views known to exist. The steam locomotives remained on the railroad until at least 1930.

In 1928, the Hoboken Manufacturers Railroad began its transition to early diesel-electric locomotives with two box cab engines. Management was so pleased with this new technology that in 1930 the railroad sold its electric motors, bringing an end to its electrified operations. In 1939 an ALCO HH600 diesel electric joined the roster and in 1949 two GE 44-ton center cab diesels were purchased. The GE 44-ton locomotives were the last motive power acquired by the railroad.

In 1954 the railroad officially adopted its nickname and became the "Hoboken Shore Railroad," continuing to operate for another two and one half decades. During that time numerous industries and warehouses moved out of Hoboken, New Jersey, leaving the railroad without a steady source of income. In the early 1960s, the railroad stopped running to its southern terminus of the New York Port Authority piers. Another serious blow occurred around 1970 when the engine house burned, which also destroyed the corporate records that were stored inside.

In the early 1970s the railroad tried to revive itself with the purchase of the former Erie Railroad business car number 4. The private car was painted dark blue with a cream window band, lettered "HBS" and was renamed "Hidden Lake." The Hoboken Shore Railroad's business car was often found sitting on a track at Fourteenth Street. This attempt to rejuvenate the railroad was short-lived. When ConRail was formed, taking over the Erie-Lackawanna Railroad, it failed to keep the tracks into Weehawken as a freight line, which drastically affected the Hoboken Shore Railroad's chances of survival. In 1978, the Hoboken Shore Railroad filed for abandonment, and in 1979 the railroad went bankrupt and liquidated all assets it still had.

*Above:* Motor No. 1 working the rails around the waterfront of Hoboken shortly after the turn of the twentieth century. The builder's plate on the motor proudly announces that it was an "Electric Locomotive manufactured by General Electric Co. in Schenectady, NY, USA." The electric motor could produce 540 horsepower. The electric motor was lettered: "Hoboken Shore Road, H.R.R.W.H.& S.S.C.Co." The abbreviation standing for the company name of Hoboken Railroad Warehouse and Steamship Connecting Company. Motor No. 1 was assisted by a tiny electric locomotive, Motor No. 2, which was constructed by General Electric Company in 1897. It sat on one truck manufactured by McGuire-Cummings Manufacturing Company. The McGuire-Cummings Manufacturing Comapny had facilities in Chicago and Paris, Illinois. (Collection of Thurlow C. Haunton, Jr.)

***Top:*** *Electric Motor No. 3 was the only electric locomotive purchased by the Hoboken Shore Road from the Baldwin Locomotive Works (builders number 28002). This forty-five ton motor was delivered in 1906. Electrical components were manufactured by Westinghouse Electric. The motor may be the only Baldwin - Westinghouse steeple cab to have a one piece cast steel frame. The expense of making a mold for such a large casting must have been considerable, but the extra weight was an advantage for pulling power. (Baldwin Locomotive Works Builders photo.).*

***Middle:*** *Motor No. 3 decked out to haul President Woodrow Wilson's train to the Hudson River, where he boarded a steamship sailing to France after World War I. The poleman on the rear is unknown. The engineer is George Donahue. Otto Voss, William Billings Sr., and an unknown railroad employee are standing on the front platform. (Collection of Thurlow C. Haunton, Jr.)*

***Bottom:*** *In 1930, Motor No. 3 was sold to the Clinton Davenport & Mascatine Railway in Iowa and renumbered to 77. In 1940, it went to the Capital Transit Company in Washington, D.C and renumbered to 054. Mr. Haunton took these two views of ex-Motor No. 3 at Benning, Washington, D.C. on July 2, 1950. The motor was soon scrapped thereafter.*

*After it left the Hoboken Shore Railroad a handbrake was installed, possibly due to the inaccessibility of its airbrake components. The hand brake can be seen in the photograph on the right. Motor No. 3 used electro-pneumatic controls rather than solenoid contactors like the General Electric motors. Electro-pneumatic controls were air powered contactors controlled by solenoid air valves and took up more room than the solenoid contactors. This explains the larger cab size of the Baldwin Locomotive Works electric locomotives. In Motor No. 3 the air compressor was housed under the hood. The small design of electric motors must have made it difficult to work on the airbrake system.*

***Top Left:*** *Motor No. 4 was manufactured by General Electric. (Collection of Thurlow C. Haunton, Jr.)*

***Top Right:*** *Steam locomotive 8, an 0-6-0 manufactured by Porter and acquired for the railroad by Brigadier General George F. Downer of the War Department from the Army. Working the yard with the steam locomotive are Motors No. 4 and No. 3. (Collection of Thurlow C. Haunton, Jr.)*

***Middle:*** *An extremely rare photograph of steam locomotive 2, an 0-6-0 acquired before 1901. The engine was scrapped in the 1920s. (Collection of Thurlow C. Haunton, Jr.)*

***Bottom:*** *Mr. Haunton may have taken the only photograph of Hoboken Manufacturers Railroad number 400, a small gas-electric locomotive manufactured by Whitcomb (Whitcomb builder's number 13098). This photograph was taken inside the railroad's engine house on August 10, 1946. In 1944 the engine was sent to Ft. Lauderdale, Florida. In May of 1946 it returned to Hoboken. A lumber company purchased the engine in the fall of 1947.*

***Top Left:*** *The Hoboken Manufacturers Railroad was at the forefront of the transition between steam powered locomotives and diesel-electric locomotives. On December 31, 1928 the railroad received box cab diesel locomotive 500 which was built by General Electric and Ingersoll Rand (builder's number 10704). This photograph captures box cab 500 sitting outside of the railroad's engine house on August 10, 1946.*

***Top Right:*** *Box cab 500 on May 26, 1945. This diesel was the first 300 horsepower, seventy ton, unit completed without parts supplied by the American Locomotive Company. Only one roof mounted General Electric CD65 type fan and Sturtevant Multivane radiator were installed.*

***Bottom:*** *Sitting in snow, box cab 500 awaits its next assignment on January 26, 1948. Less than six months after this photograph was taken the engine was retired in June, 1948. It was then sold, via Harvey LeFevre Company, New York, to the East St. Louis Stone Company in March of 1951, retaining its number. Just before its thirty-second birthday it was retired and stripped for parts by the National Museum of Transportation in St. Louis, Missouri for the restoration of Baltimore & Ohio Railroad box cab 50. The unwanted body and parts were then scrapped.*

*Top:* Box cab 600 with sweeper 350 on January 26, 1948. Delivered on the same day as her little sister, box cab 600 contained two 300 horsepower engines and weighed in at 110 tons. The GE builder's number for this unit was 10705. Big sister worked for seven more years along the Hoboken Shore Railroad than did box cab 500. It was retired in January, 1955 and sold as scrap in September, 1955, to Schiavone-Bonomo in Jersey City, New Jersey.

*Middle:* An ex-Connecticut Company work car with its motors removed provided the means to sweep away snow from the tracks during the winters. On May 26, 1945, sweeper 350 sits dormant, waiting for winter and snow to arrive. Sweeper 350 was painted red. In 1955-1956, parts from sweeper 350 were used to construct a new sweeper.

*Bottom:* Box cab 600, followed by box cab 500 and sweeper 350, sits in storage on a siding at the rear of the enginehouse. By the time this photograph was taken on July 16, 1949, box cab 600 saw relatively little usage (primarily called upon to provide power for sweeper 350) and box cab 500 was already retired.

**Top:** *Sweeper 350 sits in the snow on January 26, 1948.*

**Middle:** *In early January, 1929 a dedication ceremony was conducted to welcome the two new box cab diesel-electrics. The motive power was lined up and this photograph was taken. Pictured from right to left are: motor No. 3 &. No. 4, box cab 500 & 600 and two 0-6-0 steam locomotives, numbers 6 & 8. (Collection of Thurlow C. Haunton, Jr.)*

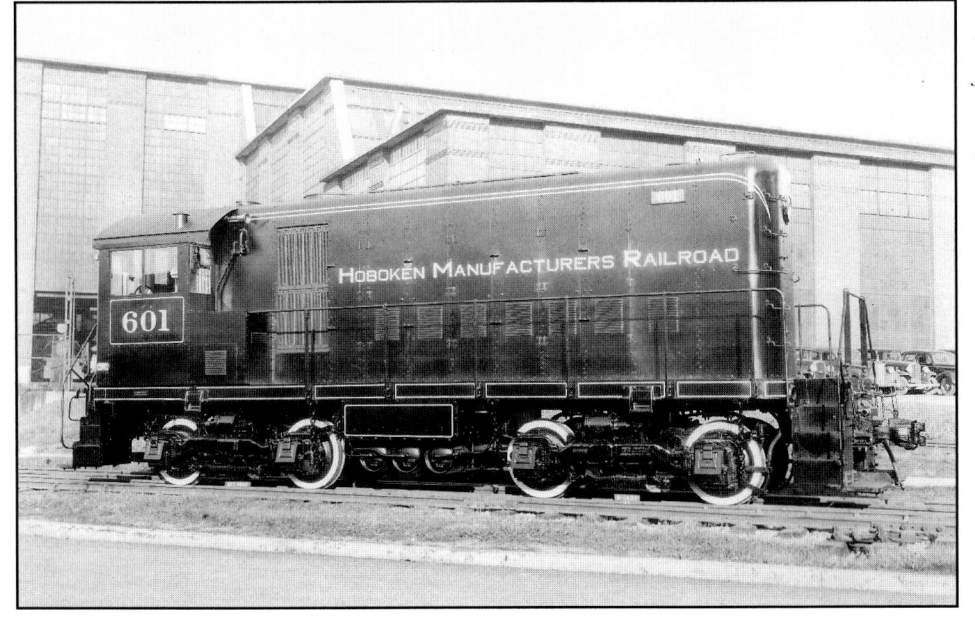

**Bottom:** *In October, 1938, ALCO manufactured an HH600, builders number 69086, for the Seatrain Lines. The HH stands for "high hood," while the 600 represents the 600 horsepower produced by the engine. Seatrain Lines had a facility along the Hoboken Manufacturers Railroad. An agreement was made between the two companies and the diesel locomotive was lettered and used by the Hoboken Manufacturers Railroad, becoming diesel 601. In December of 1946 the engine was sent by Seatrain to Edgewater, New Jersey and then to Texas at the end of 1947. (ALCO Builder's photo.)*

***Top:*** *Diesel engine 601 performing switching duties on August 10, 1946.*

***Middle Top:*** *Center cab 700 at 14th Street, Hoboken, in the snow on January 26, 1948.*

***Middle Bottom:*** *Center cab 701, coupling to a draft of box cars at 14th Street near Bloomfield Street on July 16, 1949.*

*The last motive power purchased by the Hoboken Manufacturers Railroad was two 44 ton center cab switching diesel locomotives manufactured by General Electric in Schnectady, New York. Both units were classified as class B-B88/88-4GE-733 and produced 380 horsepower. Center cab 700 was delivered on November 6, 1947 (GE builder's number 29070). Its sister, center cab 701, was constructed in October, 1947 (GE builder's number 29073).*

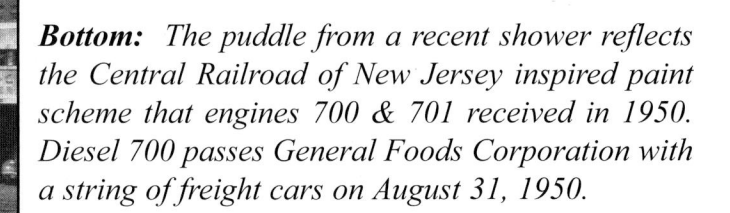

***Bottom:*** *The puddle from a recent shower reflects the Central Railroad of New Jersey inspired paint scheme that engines 700 & 701 received in 1950. Diesel 700 passes General Foods Corporation with a string of freight cars on August 31, 1950.*

***Top:*** *Diesel 700 pulls a box car away from the General Foods Corporation Franklin Baker facility on August 31, 1950. This unit was sold to the New Hope & Ivyland Railroad in Pennsylvania and was renumbered to 400. The diesel was then sold to Tyburn Railroad in Penndel and Lancaster, PA.* ***Bottom:*** *Diesel 701 switching box cars on August 31, 1950. The diesel was renumbered to 420 when the New Hope & Ivyland Railroad acquired it. It then went to the Adirondack RR and was renumbered to 107, but made its way back to the NH&I RR where it was stripped for parts.*

## HOBOKEN SHORE ROAD MOTIVE POWER ROSTER

| Number | Type of Engine | Built | Builder | Notes |
|---|---|---|---|---|
| 1 | Electric Motor | | General Electric Co. | Purchased by Hoboken Railroad Warehouse & Steamship Connecting Company. Retired circa 1928. |
| 2 | Electric Motor | 1897 | General Electric Co. | Truck manufactured by McGuire-Cummings Co. Scrapped in the 1920s. |
| 2 (2nd) | 0-6-0 Steam Loco | Circa 1901 | Porter | |
| 3 | Electric Motor | 1906 | Baldwin Locomotive | Sold to Clinton, Davenport & Mascatine Railway in 1930. To Capital Transit Company in 1940. Scrapped early 1950s. |
| 4 | Electric Motor | | General Electric Co. | Retired circa 1928. |
| 6 | Steam Locomotive | | Porter? | |
| 8 | 0-6-0 Steam Loco | | Porter? | |
| 400 | Gas-Electric | | Whitcomb | Sent to Ft. Lauderdale, FL in 1944. Returned to Hoboken in 1946. Sold to a lumber company in 1947. |
| 500 | Box Cab Diesel | 1928 | General Electric Co. | Retired in 1948 and sold via Harvey LeFevre Comapny to East St. Louis Stone Company. Stripped for parts and scrapped in 1960. |
| 600 | Box Cab Diesel | 1928 | General Electric Co. | Retired in 1955 and sold for scrap. Bell & whistle donated to NJ Transportation Heritage Center by the Billings Family in 2006. |
| 601 | Diesel Locomotive | 1938 | ALCO | Owned by Seatrain Lines; left the Hoboken Shore Road in 1946. |
| 700 | Center Cab Diesel | 1947 | General Electric Co. | Sold to New Hope & Ivyland Railroad. To Tyburn Railrod. |
| 701 | Center Cab Diesel | 1947 | General Electric Co. | Sold to New Hope & Ivyland Railroad. To Adirondack Railroad. Returned to NH&I RR and stripped for parts. |

# The Hydraulic Press Brick Company

Incorporated in 1868, the Hydraulic Press Brick Company was one of the many brick manufacturers found throughout the state of New Jersey. Today the company's primary activity is the manufacture of Haydite expanded shale lightweight aggregate, with facilities near Indianapolis, Indiana and Cleveland, Ohio.

*Above:* Hydraulic Press Brick Company steam locomotive 3, an 0-4-0, has obviously seen brighter days. The engine sits at Winslow, New Jersey in the late 1930s. (Collection of Thurlow C. Haunton, Jr.)

# The Raritan Copper Works
# The International Smelting & Refining Company

The Raritan Copper Works began processing materials in a facility in Perth Amboy, New Jersey just before the turn of the twentieth century. The works contributed to both the economic and social growth of Perth Amboy; however, these benefits did not always apply to the average worker. One of the most notable events in Raritan Copper Works history was a large riot which took place directly in front of the works.

On April 4, 1903 over four hundred laborers employed at the Raritan Copper Works went on strike and assembled in front of the works in an effort to protest their wages. The laborers were being paid $1.80 per day and were demanding a 30 cent increase in salary. When night fell, a riot broke out and it took quite some time for the local police to restore order. Four organizers of the strike were arrested and charged with rioting.

The American Smelting and Refining Company was founded in 1899 and quickly consolidated numerous works to form one large national refining company. By 1908, the company was so large and powerful that it began to dictate to its suppliers the price it would pay for raw material. Those who had interest in the Amalgamated Copper properties became disenchanted with the American Smelting and Refining Company. One of these businessmen was John D. Ryan, who along with several other associates, formed the International Smelting & Refining Company to compete with the American Smelting and Refining Company.

In March, 1911, the International Smelting & Refining Company purchased the United Metals Company's facility in Perth Amboy, New Jersey. For its plant, the United Metals Company received 40,000 shares of International Smelting & Refining Company stock, which was valued at four million dollars. Large amounts of raw materials, from as far away as Utah, were processed at the facility. In the spring of 1914, Anaconda Copper Company purchased the International Smelting & Refining Company by means of a stock exchange. Stock holders received 3.3 shares of Anaconda stock for every one share of International Smelting & Refining Company they held. The facility in Perth Amboy retained its IS&R Co. name.

The Raritan Copper Works was officially merged into the International Smelting & Refining Company (Anaconda Copper Company) in 1934. In 1976 all facilities operating under the name of the International Smelting & Refining Company in Perth Amboy closed and were liquidated.

*Above:* Pittsburgh Locomotive Works (Builder's number 46690) built this 30 inch gauge 0-4-0 saddle tank steam locomotive for the Raritan Copper Works in September, 1909. The locomotive bore the number 4. (Pittsburgh Locomotive Works Builder's Photograph.)

***Top:*** *The engineer of this fifty year old 0-4-0T Porter narrow gauge steam locomotive (number 2) gives Mr. Haunton a friendly smile at the International Smelting & Refining Company's Perth Amboy, New Jersey facility on September 23, 1955. The engine weighed a mere sixteen tons and operated on 125 pounds of steam pressure.* ***Bottom:*** *Locomotive 7 was built by Porter in 1915. This photograph of the 0-4-0T was taken on September 23, 1955.*

*Top:* Mr. Haunton was one of the lucky few railfans who had the opportunity to tour the International Smelting & Refining Company engine house. On his tour of the Perth Amboy facility on September 23, 1955, he took this image of locomotive 8 sitting inside the engine house. The engine was built by Porter in 1924.

*Bottom:* Ex-International Smelting & Refinining Company steam locomotive 9 on Pine Creek Railroad rails in Freehold, New Jesey during the summer of 1958. This 0-4-0T engine was built for the Raritan Copper Works by Porter in June, 1924 (Builder's #6916). All twenty-eight thousand pounds rested on the twenty-nine inch driving wheels, producing five thousand three hundred pounds of tractive effort. The engine operated at a boiler pressure of 170 pounds. The engine was donated to the Pine Creek RR in 1956. Today the locomotive is in a shed at Allaire State Park, NJ.

*Two additional steam locomotives Mr. Haunton photographed on his tour of the facility were engines 10 and 11. Locomotive 10 is shown above. The 0-4-0T was built by Porter in 1925. Locomotive 11 is depicted below. This Porter 0-4-0T was also constructed in 1925.*

*Top & Middle:* Two September 23, 1955, views of International Smelting & Refining Company diesel locomotive 2, which was built by Vulcan (Builder's #4712) in 1946.

*Bottom:* The sheer size difference between the thirty inch narrow gauge line engines of the refinery and that of standard equipment is clearly demonstrated by this photograph. A Pennsylvania Railroad box car towers over the dwarf gasoline fueled Plymouth engine on September 23, 1955. Engine 12 was constructed in 1925.

# The Koppers Coke Company

Henry B. Rust purchased a small coke oven company in the 1920s. Being a visionary, he approached Andrew Mellon for support and capital. Mr. Rust was soon operating a vast network of holding companies with interests in railroads, shipping, utilities and steel mills. Kopper United managed this conglomerate. Roosevelt's Public Utility Holding Company Act forced the break-up of Kopper United. The remains were named Koppers Incorporated. The company concentrated on the manufacturing of by-product coke ovens and products related to coal such as tar. A 687,990 square meter industrial site was developed in Kearny, New Jersey along the Hackensack River and was referred to as Koppers Seaboard By-product Coke Company.

The plant was razed in 1979. In 1980 the Urban Mass Transit Administration (UMTA) recommended that a heavy repair, service and inspection complex for New Jersey Transit be built on the former Koppers Coke site. The site for the proposed transit repair facility was changed in 1981 after officials learned of serious land and water contamination problems. The site sat dormant for nearly twenty years until a Remedial Action Work Plan was approved by the New Jersey Department of Environmental Protection in 1998. A steel sheet pile wall and a slurry wall were constructed to limit the discharge of contaminants into the Hackensack River. The cleanup of the site will allow it to become a commuter car storage yard in conjunction with the new trans-Hudson Express Tunnel project.

*Top: Koppers Coke 0-6-0 steam locomotive 2 working the Kearny, NJ plant in July, 1939. Replacing locomotive 2 was a Caterpillar diesel electric switcher also numbered 2 but was referred to as D 2 to prevent confusion.* **Bottom:** *In May, 1939, engine 3, an 0-4-0 saddle tanks, shifts an Erie Railroad hopper car. (Both photographs from the collection of Thurlow C. Haunton, Jr.)*

# The John Dustin's War Surplus

Although the John Dustin's War Surplus in Mt. Holly did not operate a railroad, a 4-4-0 saddle tank sat at its facility for some time. The steam locomotive was a former Philadelphia Navy Yard engine.

*Above:* Two April 26, 1966 views of the former Philadelphia Navy Yard steam locomotive sitting in the John Dustin's War Surplus facility in Mt. Holly, New Jersey. Being completely whitewashed gives the engine a unique appearance.

# The Long Beach Island Railroads

## Tuckerton Railroad

With the goal of establishing vacation resorts along the eighteen mile island known as Long Beach Island, Archelaus R. Pharo founded a corporation for the construction of Beach Haven, New Jersey. Mr. Pharo was the son of a wealthy ship builder and enjoyed spending summers on Long Beach Island. He saw the success of the Atlantic City and Cape May region and saw no reason why Long Beach Island could not enjoy that same economic growth. Before vacationers could enjoy Long Beach Island, a transportation system had to be developed. Therefore, Archelaus invested heavily into the Tuckerton Railroad.

The Tuckerton Railroad originated at Whiting, an important junction of the New Jersey Southern (Central Railroad of New Jersey) and the Pennsylvania Railroad. The railroad then traveled to Tuckerton. A short branch from Tuckerton to Edge Cove was constructed where passengers would transfer onto ferry boats, operated by the Rancocas Steamboat Company, for the journey to Beach Haven. The Tuckerton Railroad was completed in 1871.

To any large degree the traffic and operating revenue on the Tuckerton Railroad never materialized. By 1936 the railroad's financial state was in such disarray that it had to declare bankruptcy. A salvage firm from New York City purchased the line and reorganized it into the Southern New Jersey Railroad Company. In August, 1937 service between Barnegat and Tuckerton resumed. Within two years the salvage firm realized that there was more money in scrapping the line than to continue operating the railroad. In 1939 all nonessential rails were removed. In 1940 the salvage firm continued to rip up the track and scrap anything of value. On October 30, 1940 the last car load of scrap was interchanged.

## Manahawkin & Long Beach Transportation Company

The Manahawkin & Long Beach Railroad constructed a line connecting with the Tuckerton Railroad, across the Manahawkin Bay and onto Long Beach Island. The railroad was completed in 1886. Then line was operated by the Tuckerton Railroad.

## Barnegat Railroad

The railroad stretched from Barnegat City Junction to Barnegat City at the northern tip of Long Beach Island, a distance of eight miles. The Barnegat Railroad was a subsidiary of the Pennsylvania Railroad. In mid-September, 1922 the Barnegat Railroad applied to the Interstate Commerce Commission for permission to discontinue operations. The line was then leased to the Tuckerton Railroad. Within months the Tuckerton Railroad realized that the line did not offer any economic advantage to them and on June 6, 1923 the last passenger train from Surf City to Barnegat City travelled the rails. At midnight that night the Tuckerton Railroad surrendered its lease of the Barnegat Railroad.

**Author's Note**

For more information on the Tuckerton Railroad and the railroads of Long Beach Island, I highly recommend the book written by John Brinckmann on the Tuckerton Railroad.

**Right:** *The Barnegat Railroad Station at Brant Beach. (Collection of Thurlow C. Haunton, Jr.)*

***Top Left:*** *The former Brant Beach station as it appeared in January, 1959. The station has been moved across the road from its original location has been used as a residence, photo shop and storage shed.* ***Top Right:*** *A January, 1959 photograph of ex-Beach Haven station. The station was renovated into a private residence.*

***Middle:*** *Two January, 1959, views of the 12th Street Barnegat City station nearly twenty years after the rails had been removed.* ***Bottom Left:*** *The remains of the Cedar Run bridge as it appeared in June, 1959.* ***Bottom Right:*** *The wooden trestle crossing West Creek has seen better days. Photograph taken in June, 1959.*

## Whiting

**Top Three Photos:** Whiting was a junction between the Pennsylvania Railroad and the Central Railroad of New Jersey. From here the Tuckerton Railroad carried vacationers to Long Beach Island. These images depict the joint PRR-CNJ 1898 station at Whiting. The top two photographs were taken in 1955, while the photograph to the right was taken on May 1, 1948. **Middle:** Two views of an old Tuckerton Railroad passenger coach rotting away at Whiting on May 1, 1948. The coach once stood in the yards and was later used as a garage.

**Bottom Left:** The remains of the Tuckerton Railroad's water tower and shack at Whiting on May 1, 1948. **Bottom Right:** Mr. Haunton took this photograph of the abandoned turntable pit at Whitings on May 1, 1948..

## Manahawkin

**Top:** Two views of the decaying Tuckerton Railroad wooden trestle at Manahawkin on March 24, 1949.
**Middle:** The former Manahawkin station still is adorned by its telegraph call sign. Remnants of the passenger platform can also be seen in this March 25, 1948 photograph.

**Bottom:** On September 24, 1938 steam locomotive 6 works a freight at Manahawkin. This 4-4-0 was built by the Baldwin Locomotive Works (Builder's #34161) in January, 1910 and was scrapped by Bethlehem Steel in 1940. (Collection of Thurlow C. Haunton, Jr.)

*Top:* The poor condition of the wooden trestle over Cedar Creek at Bamber was documented on March 24, 1949.

*Middle:* Tuckerton Railroad locomotive 5 sits out of service at Tuckerton on October 4, 1935.  *Bottom:* In June, 1924 the Baldwin Locomotive Works (Builder's #57811) built this 4-4-0 as the Cornwall Railroad number 14.  This engine was acquired by the Tuckerton Railroad in 1930 and was scrapped at Tuckerton in 1937-38.  This October 4, 1935 view depicts the engine sitting on a siding at Tuckerton.  (Collection of Thurlow C. Haunton, Jr.)

## Tuckerton
## March 25, 1948

***Top Left:*** *An old abandoned box car body was used by the railroad as shed.* ***Top Right:*** *The small Tuckerton Railroad engine house. A turntable was once located in front of the building.* ***Middle Left:*** *This structure was once the freight house.* ***Middle Right:*** *Apparently there is no scrap value in an old water tower. When this photograph was taken the water tower had been abandoned for nearly a decade.* ***Bottom:*** *The former station at Tuckerton.*

*Top:* This small gas dinky bearing the number M-1 was built by Vulcan (Builder's #3716) in November, 1926. This April 16, 1939 photograph was taken during a rail fan excursion across the Tuckerton Railroad. *Middle:* Steam locomotive 6 pulling the April 16, 1939 excursion. *Bottom:* Locomotive 6 pulling a freight train past Tuckerton in the 1930s. (Collection of Thurlow C. Haunton, Jr.)

*Top:* Conductor George Wills, fireman Edward Ireland, engineer Archie Pharo, conductor Ed Kelly, fireman Tome Kelley, William Malsbary, and baggage master John Spencer pose with Tuckerton Railroad steam locomotive 5 at Tuckerton in 1899. This 4-4-0 was built by the Burnhams, Wms & Company (Builder's #11526) in January, 1891. Burnhams, Wms & Company was owned by the Baldwin Locomotive Works. (Collection of Thurlow C. Haunton, Jr.)

*Bottom:* This photograph taken between the years 1937 and 1940 depicts steam locomotive 5 on the turntable in front of the engine house at Tuckerton. After the New York salvage firm purchased the bankrupt Tuckerton Railroad, the railroad was reorganized and operated under the name of the Southern New Jersey Railroad, which is stenciled across the tender of the engine. (Collection of Thurlow C. Haunton, Jr.)

# The North Jersey Quarry Company, The Lakewood Sand Company, and The Porrier & McLane Contractors

Frederick Wilhelm Schmidt was born in Millington, New Jersey on August 27, 1865. At the age of twenty-three he moved to Morristown, NJ to assist his father in his carriage business. The Morris County government officials began to support and fund major improvements to the road infrastructure within the region. Being a bright businessman, Mr. Schmidt saw the protential profits that could be made by involving himself in this surge to improve public roads. In 1895 Frederick Schmidt purchased a tract of fifty acres of land in Millington, New Jersey and formed the Morris County Crushed Stone Company. The company quarried the land for trap rock to be used for road building. Within a short amount of time, Mr. Schmidt purchased several other quarries within New Jersey and New York. To consolidate his extensive quarry operations, Frederick Schmidt formed the North Jersey Quarry Company, with its headquaters in the "Schmidt Building," 15-17 South Street, Morristown, New Jersey.

*Top: In October, 1922 the Cooke Locomotive Works (American Builder's number 63296) built an 0-4-0 saddle tank steam locomotive for the North Jersey Quarry Company. When the New Jersey Turnpike was being constructed this narrow gauge locomotive was used at the Lakewood Sand Company (in South Lakewood, NJ) by turnpike contractors Porrier & McLane. This September 17, 1950 view depicts the engine in South Lakewood during the time it was being used at the Lakewood Sand Company. Bottom: Five years later Mr. Haunton returned to South Lakewood to take this view of engine 2 awaiting it fate -- the scrapper's tourch.*

# The Mount Hope Mineral Railroad

The Jackson family began mining in the Mount Hope, New Jersey area as early as 1819. A railroad was laid to assist in moving the iron ore from the mines.

*Top:* In May, 1915 the Baldwin Locomotive Works (Builder's #42076) built this 2-8-0 steam locomotive for the Mount Hope Mineral Railroad. (Baldwin Locomotive Works Builder's Photograph.)

*Bottom:* Five years after Baldwin Locomotive Works constructed engine 3, they built this 2-6-0 steam locomotive (Builder's #53947) in November, 1920. Mount Hope Mineral Railroad locomotive 4 was sold to the Middletown & Unionville Railroad in Unionville, New York, in December, 1930 and was renumbered to 5. The engine was then sold to the West Pittston - Exeter Railroad in West Pittston, Pennsylvania.

# The Morristown & Erie Railroad

During the beginning of the industrial revolution numerous mills and other industries grew up along the Whippany River near Hanover, NJ. Soon thereafter the Morris Canal and the Morris & Essex RR were constructed; however, both of these modes of transportation bypassed Hanover. The goods produced by these industries around Hanover had to be transported to market by horses and freight wagons, which was not the ideal way to transport large volumes of products. Although the idea of constructing a rail line to transport the fruits of Whippany River Valley industry had existed since the 1850s, no action was taken until the mid-1890s.

Robert McEwan, along with his seven sons, purchased several paper mills and a large cotton mill in Hanover in 1890. These mills would be later consolidated into in the McEwan Brothers Paper Board Box Company and the Whippany Paper Board Company. Large heavy freight wagons were still used to transport their products.

Seeing a need for a rail line, Mr. Melick incorporated the Whippany River Railroad in 1895. Poorly constructed and financed with short-term bonds, this four mile railroad began operations in August, 1895. The motive power was an ex-Pennsylvania Railroad 4-4-0 steam locomotive built in Altoona in December, 1884. Mr. Melick was unable to pay the bonds when they came due. The seven McEwan brothers paid the creditors and gained control of the railroad in 1896. Jesse L. McEwan became the railroad's first president. The McEwan family invested a considerable amount of capital into the rail line, rebuilding and relocating sections of the track. Two passenger trains per day were scheduled and freight extras ran as needed.

Richard McEwen, another brother, became quite involved with the day to day operations of the rail line. The railroad, as well as the old mills and the newly established industries, were thriving along the river. In fact, the railroad was turning a profit shortly after the McEwen family acquired control. Richard McEwen looked for ways to improve service and increase profitability. He decided the railroad needed to expand, and in 1902 he incorporated the Whippany & Passaic River Railroad to build a line from Whippany east to the Erie Railroad in Essex Fells. In 1903, the Whippany River Railroad and the Whippany & Passaic River Railroad were consolidated to form the Morristown & Erie Railroad. Richard McEwen became this new railroad's first president.

During the Great Depression, (combined with the death of Richard McEwan in 1936), the financial state of the Morristown & Erie Railroad began to rapidly decline. Richard's brother, Authur McEwan, took over as president and was able bring the railroad through the hard times. In 1943, Authur McEwan died and his nephew

*Above: Service began along the Morristown & Erie Railroad in 1904 using leased Erie RR locomotives as motive power. Two of these engines were numbered 993 & 1091. This leased motive power remained on the line until 1908, when Richard McEwen began to acquire motive power solely owned by the railroad. The first locomotive purchased by the M&E RR was a 2-8-0 built by Rogers (builder's number 45087) in February, 1908. M&E RR 1 was sold to the Toledo, St. Louis & Western Railroad on December 6, 1917 and was renumbered to 136. (Rogers Builder's Photo.)*

Richard W. McEwan took over as president. After World War II, traffic on M&E RR was eroding as many of the larger industries and paper mills switched from coal to oil fuel and also began to utilize tractor trailers as their prime mode for freight hauling. It was during this time that the M&E RR itself switched from steam powered locomotives to diesel engines.

By the 1970s the railroad was in a depressed state. The industries on which it had relied for three-quarters of a century were now closed or in the process of closing. Bankruptcy protection was granted in 1978 and the railroad only operated on an as-needed basis. In 1982 four men got together and purchased the bankrupt railroad. They were successful in keeping the line alive. Today the M&E Ry operates several small branches, two of which were former Central Railroad of New Jersey lines. Obtaining the switching contract for the Bayway Refinery in Linden in 1995 solidified a future for the M&E Ry. An average 8,000 freight cars are moved in, around, and out of the refinery, every year, keeping the crews of the M&E Railway quite busy.

*Top: The McEwen family was very frugal, and after the purchase of the brand new locomotive 1 the railroad purchased only used steam locomotives. This photograph depicts the remains of engine 2 at Morristown on October 12, 1935. This 2-4-4T was manufactured by the Rhode Island Locomotive Works in October, 1894, for the Chicago South Side Elevated Railroad as number 226. The Morristown & Erie Railroad acquired the engine in February, 1908. On January 1, 1922, it was sold to the Hanover Brick Company. The engine was scrapped in 1936. **Bottom:** M&E RR locomotive 7 was built as number 14 for the Lake Champlain & Moriah Railroad in 1905. The Morristown & Erie Railroad acquired the engine in January, 1917. Other engines on the M&E RR included locomotive 3, a 2-6-0 which was built in 1870 by Dickson for the DL&W RR. The M&E RR acquired it in March, 1908, and it was primarily used to switch the Whippany mills. Locomotive 4, an 0-4-4T was built by Rhode Island in 1885 as New Haven Railroad 2114. Locomotive 5 was an ex-Pennsylvania Railroad 0-6-0 B-3 class built in the Altoona Shops in the 1880's. (Both photos Collection of Thurlow C. Haunton, Jr.)*

## MORRISTOWN & ERIE RAILROAD LOCOMOTIVE ROSTER 1895-1952

| Number | Wheel Arrangement | Built | Builder | Acquired New or Used | Retired - Scrapped* | Notes |
|---|---|---|---|---|---|---|
| 1 (1st) | 4-4-0 | 8/1884 | Pennsylvania RR | 6/1895 Used | 1908* | Ex-PRR 137; Acquired by Whippany River RR |
| 1 (2nd) | 2-8-0 | 2/1908 | Rogers #45087 | New | 1917 | Sold to Toledo, St. Louis & Western on 12/16/1917 |
| 2 | 2-4-4T | 10/1894 | Rhode Island #3006 | 2/1908 Used | 1/1/1922 | ex-Chicago South Side Elevated RR 226 Sold to Hanover Brick Co., scrapped 1936 |
| 3 | 2-6-0 | 1870 | Dickson #62 | 3/1908 Used | 11/1/1927* | ex-DL&W 121 (364) |
| 4 | 0-4-4T | 1885 | Rhode Island #1557 | 6/1911 Used | 12/2/1915 | ex-New Haven 2114 Sold to General Equipment Company in 12/2/1915 |
| 5 | 0-6-0 | 1880s | Pennsylvania RR | 11/1913 Used | 1914* | ex-Pennsylvania Railroad Class B-3 |
| 6 | 2-8-0 | 5/1898 | Pittsburgh #1814 | 12/1915 Used | 12/21/1945 | ex-Pittsburgh & Lake Erie 9314 Acquired from General Equip. Co. in 12/1915 Last day of operation 12/21/1945 |
| 7 | 2-4-0 | 4/1905 | Schenectady #30749 | 1/1917 Used | 4/8&9/1952* | ex-Lake Champlain & Moriah 14 |
| 8 | 2-8-0 | 1902 | Baldwin #21178 | 5/1920 Used | 1936* | ex-Hocking Valley 244 |
| 9 | 2-8-0 | 10/1904 | Brooks #30134 | 10/1927 Used | 1/1947* | Built as Rochester & Pittsburgh 328 Purchased from Southern Iron & Equipment Co. |
| 10 | 2-8-0 | 11/1909 | Brooks #46770 | 8/1944 Used | 10/1955* | ex-Monongahela 116 |
| 11 | 2-8-0 | 7/1912 | Pittsburgh #51593 | 8/1944 Used | 1954-1955* | ex-Monongahela 131 |
| 12 | 2-8-0 | 7/1912 | Pittsburgh #51592 | 6/1946 Used | 10/1955 | ex-Monongahela 130 |
| 14 | Model S4 Diesel | 4/1952 | ALCO-GE #79786 | New | 3/1986 | Named "Mauritius Jensen" Sold to Linden Chlorine in 3/1986 |

*Top:* Steam locomotive 7 in storage at Morristown on November 8, 1947.  *Bottom:* Stripped of her tender, engine 7 sits on a small piece of panel track awaiting the scrapper's torch.  Photograph taken on January 26, 1948.

109

*Top:* *Locomotive 9 at Whippany on June 29, 1946. This engine was originally Buffalo, Rochester & Pittsburgh RR 328 and was built by Brooks in October, 1904. The M&E RR acquired the engine in 1927 and scrapped it nearly twenty years later in January, 1947.*

*Bottom:* *Locomotive 10 at Whippany in 1946. This engine was ex-Monongahela Railroad 116 and was purchased in August, 1944.*

***Top:*** *Steam locomotive 10 works on February 2, 1951. The crew would find some comfort in the cab on this cold winter day.*

***Bottom:*** *Locomotive 11 at work at Hanover, New Jersey on December 26, 1946.*

***Top:*** *Within days of this December 19, 1953 photograph, locomotive 11 was sold for scrap. The engine was ex-Monongahela RR 131 and was purchased by the M&E RR in August, 1944.*

***Bottom:*** *Working hard, steam locomotive 12 pulls a freight across a public highway at Beaufort on February 2, 1951.*

***Top:*** *The last steam locomotive purchased by the Morristown & Erie Railroad was engine 12 in June, 1946. Steam locomotive 12 was sold for scrap in October, 1955, bringing the age of regular steam powered freight trains to a close on the Morristown & Erie Railroad.*

***Bottom:*** *On February 2, 1951, Mr. Haunton captured this view of steam locomotive 12 switching a freight train at Whippany, New Jersey.*

*Top:* Steam locomotive 12 with a freight train at Whippany on February 28, 1948.

*Middle :* Caboose 1 was built in 1884 and served the Delaware, Lackawanna & Western Railroad as caboose 4. The Morristown & Erie Railroad acquired the caboose in 1933. This photograph depicts caboose 1 on December 30, 1949. Today the caboose is preserved at the Whippany Railway Museum, Whippany, New Jersey, and is owned by the United Railroad Historical Society of New Jersey.

*Bottom:* Rail crane 5 sits at Morristown on August 10, 1946. The crane was built by the Terry Contracting Locomotive Crane Company in 1922 and was used along the M&E RR until 1940. It sat rusting for ten years before being scrapped.

*Top:* In January, 1914, the Morristown & Erie Railroad purchased combine 5129 from the Pennsylvania Railroad. By the time Mr. Haunton took this photograph on April 23, 1945 the wooden combine was in a sad state. Fire consumed the combine's remains on April 5, 1946.

*Middle & Bottom:* Two December 19, 1953 views of the Morristown & Erie Railroad enginehouse with caboose 1 and steam locomotive 11 siting in the yard.

*Top:* Recently purchased NYS&W caboose 0101 sits at the Morristown & Erie Railroad shop facilities on July 16, 1949. *Middle:* After receiving some repairs and a new coat of paint the former NYS&W caboose became M&E RR caboose 2. With snow about his feet, Mr. Haunton braved the elements and was rewarded with a passing M&E RR freight train at Whippany on February 2, 1951. Locomotive 12 was at the front of the train and caboose 2 brought up the rear. *Bottom:* Locomotive 12 and the M&E RR shops on August 10, 1946.

*Top:* Two views of diesel 14 at Whippany on December 19, 1953. This ALCO - General Electric 1000 horsepower diesel (Builder's number 79786) was built for the M&E RR in April, 1952. The engine was named "Mauritus Jensen." In March, 1986 it was sold to Linden Chlorine.

*Middle:* An ALCO RS-1 served the Morristown & Erie Railroad as diesel 15. The left photograph depicts the diesel with a train at Whippany on April 16, 1955. In the right photograph diesel 15 pulls a freight train with caboose 2 out in front as it passes through Whippany on February 26, 1966. In 1985 diesel 15 was sold to the Valley RR in Essex, CT.

*Bottom:* This December 19, 1953 photograph shows the M&E RR station at Morristown being used as an office for a local coal company. Behind the station was the Greenson Paper Mill. The M&E RR flourished in its younger days, providing transportation for paper mills and other industries which grew up along the Whippany River.

# The New York Shipbuilding Corporation

In 1899 the New York Shipbuilding Corporation was founded, opening its first shipyard in Camden, New Jersey in 1900. Between 1900 and 1967 the company built more then five hundred vessels for the United States military and for other maritime customers. The last civilian vessel, the S.S. Export Adventurer, was launched in 1960. The last military vessel ordered was the USS Camden for the Navy in 1967. Today the former shipyard is now part of the Port of Camden and is used for handling breakbulk cargo.

*Above:* Thurlow C. Haunton, Jr. took this photograph of New York Shipbuilding Company 0-4-0T steam locomotive X-2284 on July 8, 1957. This little saddle tank was manufactured by Vulcan (Builder's #4261) in 1939.

# The Port Reading Creosoting Plant

On November 5, 1890 the Port Reading Railroad Company was incorporated. The rail line was built from Bound Brook, New Jersey to Arthur Kill on the northern tidewaters of the New Jersey coast. The Port Reading Railroad entered into an operating agreement with the Philadelphia & Reading Railroad on September 1, 1892. Using the Port Reading Railroad as a cover, the P&R Railroad circumvented a New Jersey state law and leased the Central Railroad of New Jersey. A year later the P&R Railroad was ordered by the New Jersey legislature to terminate its lease with the CRRofNJ. Although the P&R Railroad was unsuccessful in controlling the Central Railroad of New Jersey, the two railroads went together and constructed a large creosoting facility at the tidewater terminus of the line. This creosoting facility became known as the Port Reading Creosoting plant.

*Top: To move the lumber around the creosoting plant a 36 inch narrow gauge railroad was used. On August 27, 1949, Mr. Haunton took this photograph of locomotive 2 taking on water. This engine was manufactured by H.K. Porter (Builder's #2817) in 1903 for the Barber Asphalt Company. The engine was sold for scrap in January, 1955. Assisting at the plant was locomotive 1, a Vulcan saddle tank engine. Bottom: Engine 3 was diesel locomotive manufactured by Brookville using a Caterpillar diesel engine.*

# The R. M. Hollingshead Company

The R. M. Hollingshead company maintained a large industrial plant in Camden, New Jersey. The company manufactured floor wax, furniture polish, paint, cigarette lighter fluid and other flammable products. Today the R. M. Hollingshead Company is still remembered by the older generation of Camden primary due to the devastating fire and explosions that rocked the city on July 30, 1940. A large portion of the company buildings were destroyed that dry and hot summer day. Two hundred people were injured, several of them mortally, and over two million dollars of damage to the plant and the surrounding Camden community occurred.

*Above:* A gas powered Plymouth engine provided the horsepower to move material around the R. M. Hollingshead Company in Camden, New Jersey. This view of the engine was taken in the summer of 1961.

# The Rahway Valley Railroad

Operations this line began in 1897 under the name of the New York & Orange Railroad. The line extended from Kenilworth to Aldene, New Jersey and interchanged with the Lehigh Valley Railroad at Roselle Park and the Central Railroad of New Jersey at Cranford. The railroad's name was soon changed to the New Orange Four Junction Railroad. (Coming no doubt from the fact that the line had four junctions.) Louis Keller, well-known Social Register publisher and co-founder of the Baltusrol Golf Club acquired the line in 1904. In 1905 the railroad's name was changed to the Rahway Valley Railroad.

Mr. Keller immediately extended the railroad past the golf club to Summit, New Jersey and came within a few feet of the Delaware, Lackawanna & Western Railroad; however, a connection with the DL&W was not made until 1931. A station was constructed at the golf club and at one time was listed in the Official Guide. The Baltusrol post office soon took residence in the station building. Fourteen passenger trains were operated on the line. This number dwindled to six by 1909. In 1919 the railroad gave up passenger service altogether and became a freight only line. A three mile branch to Maplewood, near Newark, was constructed in 1911.

Louis Keller died in 1921, leaving the railroad in poor physical and financial shape. Shortly before his death Roger Clark took over managerial responsibilities. Mr. Clark was an experienced railroader who had worked for the Buffalo, Rochester & Pittsburgh Railroad and the Central Railroad of Oregon. Mr. Clark's son, Geroge Clark became the railroad's traffic manager. Roger Clark died in 1932 and his son George took over as president. Following in his father's footsteps, he slowly turned the Rahway Valley Railroad into a profitable enterprise. The railroad's first profit came at the height of the Great Depression in 1934, a feat which should be commended.

According to an interview of George Clark by John T. Cumningham in 1950 for Trains Magazine, the Rahway Valley Railroad functioned with twenty-one employees: "One train crew - engineer, fireman, conductor and two brakeman - a section crew of six, three agents, two men in the shop, and the rest of us here in the office." Mr. Clark also pointed out that the office personnel were sometimes required to work out along the railroad. This was the case during the blizzard of December 26, 1947.

A typical day of operations for the railroad, during the early 1950s was for the crew to leave Kenilworth at 8:30 AM and travel to Aldene, pick up northbound cars, and spend the rest of the day drilling over the line to Summit and Maplewood before retiring for the day back at Kenilworth. There were two main obstacles along the Rahway Valley line. First, the grade-crossing over Route 22 was referred to as "The Gauntlet." Even president Clark made remarks regarding his fears of this grade crossing. The second obstacle was the steep grade into Summit. The three Baldwin steam locomotives used for years could not handle more than eight

***Above:*** *Possibly the only brand new steam locomotive the Rahway Valley Railroad purchased, engine 7, arrived on the line in 1908. This locomotive was sold and shipped to Spain in the 1920s. (Baldwin Builder's Photo.)*

loaded cars up the three-mile grade. The railroad also handled less-than-car load freight. It was not uncommon to see several boxes of merchandise strapped to the pilot beam of the steam locomotive. Since the railroad did not own any box cars of its own, it was cheaper to carry less-than-car-load freight on the engine.

In 1950 approximately 40 percent of the Rahway Valley Railroad's traffic was anthracite coal. Within a few years anthracite tonnage dropped considerably and the railroad's revenue fell sharply. The railroad limped through the 1960s; however, with the formation of Conrail on April 1, 1976 the railroad's fate was sealed. Conrail consolidated the interchange of all freight at Cranford, eliminating Summit on the former Erie-Lackawanna line. The Rahway Valley Railroad was purchased by the Delaware Ostego Corporation. The last movement over the Rahway Valley line occurred on April 21, 1992. The trip originated at the Kenilworth enginehouse and slowly crept along the line to the ex-Central Railroad of New Jersey interchange at Cranford. Much of the Rahway Valley was recently rebuilt but funding ran out and service has not been restored on the disconencted track segments.

## RAHWAY VALLEY RAILROAD STEAM LOCOMOTIVE ROSTER

| Number | Wheel Arrangement | Built | Builder | Notes |
|---|---|---|---|---|
| 1 | 4-4-0 | | | ex-Northern Central 322 |
| 2 | | | | |
| 3 | 4-4-0 | | | ex-Lehigh Valley, wrecked in 1906 |
| 4 | 2-6-0 | | | ex-Lackawanna |
| 5 | 0-6-0 | 8/1882 | Baldwin #6305 | ex-Central Railroad of New Jersey 23 (710) |
| 6 | | | | |
| 7 | 2-4-4 | 1908 | Baldwin #32817 | Sold to General Equip. Co., shipped to Spain |
| 8 | 2-8-0 | 1900 | Pittsburgh #2070 | ex-P&LE, acquired 1916, scrapped 4/1929 |
| 9 | 0-6-0 | 11/1893 | PRR Altoona | ex-PRR, acquired 1917, scrapped 1920s |
| 10 | 0-6-0 | 11/1893 | PRR Altoona | ex-PRR, acquired 1917, scrapped 1920s |
| 11 | 2-6-0 | 3/1904 | Baldwin | ex-Grafton & Upton 5, acquired 1920 |
| 12 | 2-8-0 | | Pittsburgh | ex-Bessemer & Lake Erie 96, acquired 1927, retired 1929, scrapped 2/1943 |
| 13 | 2-8-0 | 9/1905 | Baldwin #26355 | ex-L&NE 19, acquired 1929 |
| 14 | 2-8-0 | 9/1905 | Baldwin #26356 | ex-L&NE 20, acq. 1929, scrapped 12/1951 |
| 15 | 2-8-0 | 3/1916 | Baldwin #43529 | ex-Oneida & Western 20, on display at Steamtown, Scranton, PA |

*Top:* Steam locomotive 7 at work along the Rahway Valley Railroad. (Thurlow C. Haunton, Jr. Collection.)

*Middle:* This circa 1920 photograph depicts locomotive 8 at Kenilworth. The Pittsburgh Locomotive Works built this 2-8-0 locomotive in 1900 for the Pittsburgh & Lake Erie Railroad. The Rahway Valley acquired the locomotive in 1916. In April, 1929, the steam locomotive was scrapped. (Thurlow C. Haunton, Jr. Collection.)

*Bottom:* Grafton & Upton Railroad locomotive 5 was acquired by the Rahway Valley in 1920 and was renumbered to number 11. On August 11, 1934, the locomotive sits at Kenilworth. (Thurlow C. Haunton, Jr. Collection.)

*Top:* Engine 12 at the Rahway Valley Railroad's facilities in Kenilworth. (Thurlow C. Haunton, Jr. Collection.)

*Bottom:* Rahway Valley Railroad locomotives 13 & 14, acquired in 1929, were ex-Lehigh & New England engines built by the Baldwin Locomotive Works in September, 1905. Lehigh & New England engine 19 became engine 13 on the Rahway Valley Railroad. ( Baldwin Builder's Photograph.).

*Top:* Locomotive 13 has just climbed the three-mile grade to Summit to interchange with the Lackawanna. Note the box of less-than-car-load freight on the front pilot board. (Thurlow C. Haunton, Jr. Collection.)  *Bottom:* On June 29, 1949, locomotive 13 has just taken on water before steaming out of Kenilworth to begin the day's work.

***Top:*** *Rahway Valley Railroad 10 was a gasoline combine built by the Railway Motor Car Corporation in Philadelphia in 1910. Its life along the Rahway Valley was short lived. (Railway Motor Car Corporation Builder's photograph.)*

***Middle:*** *In December, 1937 the Rahway Valley acquired Onieda & Western locomotive 20. (Baldwin Builder's Photograph.)* ***Bottom:*** *Apparently the Rahway Valley would rotate their steam locomotives in and out of service on a monthly basis. On February 8, 1951 engine 13 pushes engine 15 back into the enginehouse.*

*Top:* Rahway Valley Steam locomotive 15 works at Kenilworth.

*Middle:* On July 16, 1949 locomotive 15 is heading to Summit. The train crew members standing and sitting on the front pilot add a unique flavor to this image. They must feel comfortable out in front considering the limited speed of the train as it ascends the stiff grade into Summit.

*Springfield*

*Roselle Park*

**Thurlow C. Haunton Jr.'s Visit to the Rahway Valley Railroad on January 19, 1951**

**Steam Locomotive 15 in action**

*Roselle Park*

128

*Aldene*

*Aldene*

*Aldene*

# RAHWAY VALLEY RAILROAD DIESEL LOCOMOTIVE ROSTER

| Number | Built | Builder | Horsepower | Notes |
|--------|-------|---------|------------|-------|
| 16 | 1/1951 | General Electric #30838 | 600 | Currently both diesels are owned by the United Railroad Historical Society of NJ and are leased to Whippany Railway Museum. |
| 17 | 1/1954 | General Electric #32130 | 600 | |

*Top:* Diesel locomotive 16 at Roselle Park on April 10, 1951. The diesel arrived on the railroad on January 29, 1951.
*Bottom:* The railroad's second diesel locomotive, engine 17, joined the roster on February 2, 1954. The engine was less than a month old when Mr. Haunton took this photograph at Roselle Park on February 22, 1954.

***Top:*** *As engine 16 pushed diesel locomotive 17 into the Rahway Valley Railroad's enginehouse at Kenilworth in July, 1957, the crew on their pilots give Mr. Haunton a grin. Inside the enginehouse, a two track wooden building, the railroad performed minor repairs on its engines. If a steam locomotive needed major repairs it was sent to the Lackawanna Railroad's facilities at Kingsland.*

***Bottom:*** *Caboose 102 sits at Kenilworth on June 25, 1949. The railroad purchased the caboose from the Lackawanna Railroad in 1934.*

# The Raritan River Sand Company

Taking advantage of New Jersey's abundance of sand the Raritan River Sand Company was formed and operated out of Nixon, New Jersey. The sand company maintained a fleet of narrow gauge locomotives.

***Top:*** *Raritan River Sand Company locomotive 4 was used by the Pine Creek Railroad until it was sold to Disneyland in Anahime, California in August, 1958. This 0-4-0 steam locomotive was built by the Baldwin Locomotive Works (Builder's #58367) in April, 1925.* ***Bottom:*** *Raritan River Sand Comapny locomotive 3 provided the motive power for the Cranberry Creek Railroad, a rail line within a tourist theme park known as Cowboy City in Howell, New Jersey between the years 1957 and 1959. Originaly built as a tank engine by Porter (Builer's #6932) in 1924 for the Hope Natural Gas Company in Pittsburgh, the engine was soon thereafter sold to the Raritan River Sand Comapny. The engine was used by the sand company until 1956 when it was purchased by James Wright and Jay Wulfson. These two men had founded the Pine Creek Railraod in 1952. In 1960 the locomotive was sold to the Busch Woodlands Museum in Copperstown, New York. The Great Excape Fun Park purchased the engine in 1971. The Orlando Internation Toy Train Museum acquired the steam locomotive in 1990. In 1995 it was moved to a museum in Agrirama, Georgia.*

# The Sandy Hook Proving Grounds

Developed on an 1665 acre barrier beach peninsula located at the northern tip of the New Jersey Shore, Sandy Hook Proving Grounds and Fort Hancock were constructed to protect the entrance into the New York Harbor. The Hook was first fortified by the United States Army during the War of 1812. The proving grounds tested ammunitions and weapons. The military ceased its operation on Sandy Hook in 1974. Today, the remains of the proving ground and Fort Hancock are part of a National Recreation Area.

***Top:*** *This 0-4-0T was manufactured by the Pittsburgh Locomotive Works (Builder's #2323) for the Sandy Hook Proving Grounds in May, 1901. (Pittsburgh Locomotive Works Builder's Photograph.)* ***Bottom:*** *In 1904 the Baldwin Locomotive Works (Builder's #23969) built Sandy Hook Proving Grounds locomotive 4, which was named "General Rodman. (Baldwin Locomotive Works Builder's Photograph.)*

*Above:* Steam locomotive 5 joined the Sandy Hook Proving Grounds roster in July, 1913. The 2-4-0 was built by the Baldwin Locomotive Works (Builder's #40217). (Baldwin Locomotive Works Builder's Photograph.)

# The Sayer & Fisher Brick Company

The Sayer & Fisher Brick Company was one of several brick manufacturers that were located in New Jersey. The brick company maintained a 37 inch narrow gauge railroad. Throughout the company's history, eight 0-4-0 saddle tank engines and two gas powered Plymouth engines were used.

*Above:* Mr. Haunton took this photograph of Sayer & Fisher Brick Company steam locomotive 2 in front of its two gas powered Plymouth engines inside their engine house in 1954.

# Standard Oil Company of New Jersey

John D. Rockefeller involved himself in oil refining within the state of New Jersey during the 1870s. To take advantage of New Jersey laws, which allowed corporations to own stock in other companies, John D. Rockefeller formed the Standard Oil Company of New Jersey in 1882. Primarily this was a holding corporation for other companies who in turn owned other firms; however, Standard Oil did have several large facilities within the state.

## Bayonne Works

In 1875 an oil refinery was built on Constable Hook, Bayonne, where Kill Von Kull meets the Upper New York Bay. Standard Oil acquired control of this refinery in 1877. The Bayonne Works was the first of the Standard Oil tidewater facilities to be directly connected to the oil fields by a pipeline in 1881.

*Above:* Standard Oil Company of New Jersey, Bayonne Works 0-6-0 steam locomotive 4 was built by Baldwin Locomotive Works (Builder's number 41588) in 1914. (Baldwin Locomotive Works Builder's Photograph.)

## Bayway Refinery

Mr. Rockefeller began purchasing large tracts of land between Linden and Elizabeth, New Jersey for the construction of a Standard Oil refinery shortly after the turn of the twentieth century. Construction of this refinery, formally known as the Bayway Refinery, was completed in 1909. The refinery was located on the Arthur Kill. When the refinery opened, twenty thousand barrels of crude oil were being processed each day. When the Standard Oil Company on New Jersey was broken up by antitrust laws, it became Esso and the refinery was renamed the Esso Refinery. Today the facility is known as the Bayshore Terminal Company, and the Morristown & Erie Railway handles the switching of eight thousand rail cars a year.

*Above:* Joining the Bayway Refinery locomotive roster in November of 1912 was this tiny 0-4-0 saddle tank. The locomotive was built by the Baldwin Locomotive Works (Builder's number 38830). (Baldwin Locomotive Works Builder's Photo.)

# The United States Army -- Fort Dix

In 1917 thirty-one thousand acres of farmland and forest in the Pinelands of New Jersey were transformed into an Army base known at Fort Dix. The Union Transportation Company (see volume 1) brought supplies and transported troops to and from the base. On the grounds of the base a 23 5/8 inch narrow gauge railroad was constructed. A gas powered Plymouth built in 1936 provided motive power until the narrow gauge line was abandoned in 1948. A standard gauge rail line was also constructed to interchange with the Union Transportation Company. Today the installation is primary used for the training of Army reserves.

*Above: United States Army 8653 sits at the Fort Dix engine house on April 10, 1958. This diesel locomotive was built for the Army by ALCO - General Electric.*

# The Warren Foundry and Machine Company

On March 3, 1856 the Warren Foundry and Machine Company was formed with the intention of conducting general foundry activities. The foundry's facilities were located in Phillipsburg, New Jersey. Two English foundrymen, John Firth and John Ingham, joined the company in 1857 and, using their expertise, the company began manufacturing thirty inch pipe in dry sand pit molds. This process was applied to smaller size pipe and from then on the company's main purpose was the manufacturing of cast iron piping. In 1951 the plant was modernized and the method of manufacturing pipe was changed to centrifugal casting using metal molds.

The foundry was purchased several times and has operated under the names Shamoon Industries and Canron Industries. In 1975 the plant ownership once again changed and the name of the foundry was changed to Atlantic States Cast Iron Pipe Company, a division of McWane, Incorporated. Today the company is regarded as one of the premier manufacturers of Ductile Iron pipe.

*Above: Three views of Warren Foundry & Machine Co. locomotive 7, a 0-4-0T built by Vulcan (Builder's #4209) in 1937, sitting at the company's facility in Phillipsburg, New Jersey on July 1, 1958.*

# Additional Builder's Photographs

*Top:* This 0-6-0T named "Gregory" was manufactured by the Schnectady Locomotive Works (Builder's #2706) for the North River Coal & Wharf Company in 1888. The company was located in Jersey City. (Schnectady Builder's Photo.) *Middle:* In October, 1890 the Baldwin Locomotive Works (Builder's #11275) built the "William A" for the North River Coal & Wharf Company. The Baldwin Locomotive Works built three additional 0-6-0T steam locomotives for this company. They included "George J. Jr." built in 1887 (Builder's #5760), "Jefferson R.," and the "Thomas H." built in November, 1922 (builder's #55734). (Baldwin Builder's Photo.) *Bottom:* In June, 1918 the Baldwin Locomotive Works (Builder's #49090) delivered engine 3 to the Navel Ammunition Depot in Dover, New Jersey. (Baldwin Builder's Photo.)

139

***Top:*** *Steam locomotive 9 was constructed by the Baldwin Locomotive Works (Builder's #33106) in January, 1909 for the Wharton Steel Company in Wharton, New Jersey. In December, 1919 the locomotive was acquired by the Wharton & Northern Railroad and was renumbered to engine 27. The 0-6-0T was scrapped by the Bethlehem Steel Company in April, 1931. (Baldwin Builder's Photograph.)*

***Bottom:*** *This forty-five ton three hundred horsepower diesel locomotive was built by General Electric (Builder's #31299) in March, 1952 for the Worthington Pump & Machinery Corporation. Henry R. Worthington founded this company in 1845. In 1904 the company moved from its cramped Brooklyn, New York facilities to a commodious modern manufacturing plant in Harrison, New Jersey. By 1928 over three miles of standard-gauge railroad trackage was laid to service the plant's needs. (General Electric Builder's Photograph.)*